WHIZ KIDS
TELL ME WHAT THE TIME IS

Written and
illustrated by
SHIRLEY WILLIS

BOOK HOUSE

WHAT IS TIME?

Time goes by.
You can't see it,
but time is always
moving on.

We sleep at night,
but time never stops.
It moves on all
through the day and
all through the night.
As you read these
words, time has
moved on.

AS WE SLEEP, TIME MOVES US ON...

YESTERDAY

The day that has just gone by is called yesterday.

TODAY

The day that is happening now is called today.

TOMORROW

The day that is coming is called tomorrow.

...INTO THE NEXT DAY!

WHERE DOES TIME GO?

When time goes by,
it's gone forever.
Time never comes back
– it moves on.

THE PAST

The past is over.
It is time that
has gone by.

THE PRESENT

The present is time
that is happening
now.

THE FUTURE

The future is time
that is going
to happen.

I REMEMBER THE PAST!

WHEN I GROW UP...

You can plan the future, but you can never be sure how it will turn out.

I LIVE IN THE PRESENT!

I DREAM ABOUT THE FUTURE!

When time passes, it moves forward into the future.

9

HAS TIME GONE BY?

A clock tells you
that time has gone by.
Your body tells you too.

BODY CLOCK

Your body reminds
you about time:
your tummy rumbles
when it's time to eat.
You can't stop yawning
when it's time to sleep.

We see time go by as daytime turns into night-time.

FOLLOW THE SUN

Stand a stick up in a flowerpot full of soil. Now place the pot in a sunny spot in the playground. Draw a chalk line around the shadow of the stick.
Do this once every hour.
What happens to the shadow?

As the day goes by, the shadow keeps moving as the Sun moves across the sky.

Each day the Sun rises, moves across the sky and then sets. The Sun is like a clock that measures out daytime hours. Before clocks were invented, people used the Sun to tell the time.

11

WHY DOES TIME GO SLOWLY?

Time never goes faster or slower – it only seems to. Time always goes at exactly the same speed.

SHOPPING TAKES FOREVER!

Time never goes slowly, but it seems never-ending when you're bored.

THERE'S NEVER ENOUGH TIME!

WHOOSH!

SEE FOR YOURSELF

Use a small hourglass to try this experiment.

1. Turn the hourglass upside down. Play a game with your friends in the playground until the sand runs out. Did time go by quickly?
2. Turn the hourglass upside down. Now stand still like statues until the sand runs out. Did time go by much slower?

Each time, the hourglass measured out the same amount of time.

Time never goes fast, but it seems to when you're having fun.

IS IT TIME YET?

We need to know about time.
It helps us do things
on the right day and
at the right time.

IS IT
LUNCHTIME?

IS IT A
SCHOOL DAY?

IS IT TIME
FOR A WALK?

It is better to be on time
– not early or late.

WHAT DAY IS IT?

There are seven days in a week.
Each day has a name
and a place in the week.

THE WEEK ALWAYS STARTS WITH MONDAY!

MONDAY

TUESDAY

WEDNESDAY

THURSDAY

When seven days go by, a new week begins. We start with the first day all over again.

HOW DO YOU SPEND YOUR TIME?

Write down the days of the week in order.
Now think of what you do each day.
Do you do anything at the same time each day?
Do you do anything at the same time each week?

SATURDAY AND SUNDAY ARE CALLED THE WEEKEND!

FRIDAY

SATURDAY

SUNDAY

5 6

How Long Is A Day?

A day is 24 hours long.
Some hours are in the day
and some are at night.
In each day there is
daytime and night-time.

The day starts long
before you wake up.
Each new day begins
at midnight.

IT'S THE BEGINNING OF THE DAY, BUT... IT'S THE MIDDLE OF THE NIGHT!

Each new day begins when you are fast asleep in bed.

HOW LONG IS AN HOUR?

An hour is quite a long time.
Lunchtime is usually
one hour long.

We divide each
hour into small
equal parts called
minutes. There are
60 minutes in
each hour.

20

How Much Time Is Left?

IT ONLY TOOK US 5 MINUTES TO EAT THE CAKE!

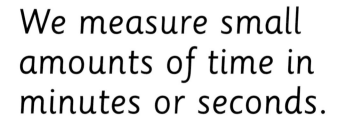

We measure small amounts of time in minutes or seconds.

A minute goes by quickly – it's not much time.

A second goes by more quickly – it's even less time.

JUST A MINUTE!

How long is a minute?
Guess how many times you can
clap your hands, bounce a ball
or jump in one minute.
Ask an adult to time you.

JUST A SECOND!

How long is a second?
Put your hand on your chest
to feel your heartbeat.
The time between each heartbeat
is about one second long.

THUMP!

THUMP!

23

WHAT TIME IS IT?

Clocks measure time for us
in hours and minutes.
We look at a clock to see
how much time has gone by
and how much time
is left.

THE HANDS
of THE CLOCK...

WHEN BOTH HANDS
POINT TO 12,
IT IS 12 O'CLOCK!

The big hand points
to each minute
that goes by.

24

WHAT TIME OF YEAR IS IT?

There are four seasons
in each year – spring,
summer, autumn and winter.
Each season brings changes
as the year goes by.

SPRING

Lots of shoots
and buds begin
to grow in spring.

SUMMER

The days are warm
and school closes
in summer.

AUTUMN

The leaves change
colour and fall from
the trees in autumn.

WINTER

The days are cold,
but winter can be
lots of fun.

WHAT GOES AROUND AND AROUND?

You will need:

- 2 pieces of cardboard (about 20 cm x 20 cm)
- 1 paper plate (20 cm)
- A ruler
- Felt-tip pens
- 1 paper fastener
- Scissors

1. Draw 2 lines on each piece of cardboard.
2. Put the paper plate on top of each piece and draw around it.
3. Cut the circles out (ask an adult to help).
4. Cut a piece out of one circle only.
5. Do one drawing for each season on the other circle.
6. Join the circles together in the centre with a paper fastener.

1.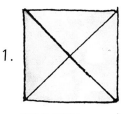
2.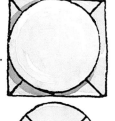
3.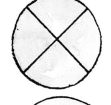
4.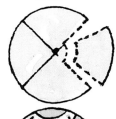
5.
6.

WHEN WINTER ENDS, SPRING COMES AROUND AGAIN!

Turn the top circle. See how the seasons keep changing.

27

IS A YEAR A LONG TIME?

THE MONTHS OF THE YEAR

A year is 365 days long.

We divide each year into twelve parts called months.

JANUARY

FEBRUARY

MARCH

APRIL

MAY

JUNE

JULY

AUGUST

SEPTEMBER

OCTOBER

NOVEMBER

DECEMBER

A month is about 30 days long. Each month has its own name and place in the year.

WHAT COMES NEXT?

Every day, week and month of the year is marked on a calendar.
Calendars help us plan time.

28

MARCH

Emma

Wendy

Jonathan

HAPPY BIRTHDAY!

A BIRTHDAY TIME LINE

You will need: 12 squares of thin cardboard
(about 15 cm x 15 cm)
Some drawing pins
Coloured felt-tip pens

1. There are 12 months in a year.
   Write the name of one month
   on each square of cardboard.
   (Use one square for each month.)
2. When is your birthday?
   Find the right month and write
   your name on that square.
   Ask everyone in your class to do
   the same.
3. Now pin all the squares to the wall.
   (Make sure that the months are
   in the right order – see page 28.)

29

GLOSSARY

calendar A chart showing every day, week and month in a year in the right order in time.

clock A device to measure time.

day A unit of time that is 24 hours long.

early Before the planned time.

hour A unit of time that is 60 minutes long.

late After the planned time.

midnight 12 o'clock at night – it is when each new day begins.

minute A unit of time that is 60 seconds long.

month One of the 12 parts that make up a year.

night The part of each day between sunset and sunrise.

season Part of a year – each season is about 3 months long.

second A very small unit of time.

week A unit of time that is 7 days long.

weekend Saturday and Sunday.

year A unit of time that is 365 days long. It is the same as 52 weeks or 12 months.

30